LADYBUG

David M. Schwartz is an award-winning author of children's books, on a wide variety of topics, loved by children around the world. Dwight Kuhn's scientific expertise and artful eye work together with the camera to capture the awesome wonder of the natural world.

Please visit our web site at: www.garethstevens.com
For a free color catalog describing Gareth Stevens Publishing's list of high-quality books
and multimedia programs, call 1-800-542-2595 (USA) or 1-800-461-9120 (Canada).
Gareth Stevens Publishing's Fax: (414) 332-3567.

Library of Congress Cataloging-in-Publication Data

Schwartz, David M.
    Ladybug / by David M. Schwartz; photographs by Dwight Kuhn. — North American ed.
        p. cm. — (Life cycles: a springboards into science series)
    Includes bibliographical references and index.
    ISBN 0-8368-2977-8 (lib. bdg.)
    1. Ladybugs—Life cycles—Juvenile literature. [1. Ladybugs.] I. Kuhn, Dwight, ill.
    II. Title.
    QL596.C65S38   2001
    595.76'9—dc21   2001031458

This North American edition first published in 2001 by
Gareth Stevens Publishing
A World Almanac Education Group Company
330 West Olive Street, Suite 100
Milwaukee, WI 53212 USA

First published in the United States in 1999 by Creative Teaching Press, Inc., P.O. Box 2723, Huntington Beach, CA 92647-0723.
Text © 1999 by David M. Schwartz; photographs © 1999 by Dwight Kuhn. Additional end matter © 2001 by Gareth Stevens, Inc.

Gareth Stevens editor: Mary Dykstra

1 2 3 4 5 6 7 8 9 05 04 03 02 01

LADYBUG

by David M. Schwartz
photographs by Dwight Kuhn

A SPRINGBOARDS INTO

SCIENCE

SERIES

Gareth Stevens Publishing
A WORLD ALMANAC EDUCATION GROUP COMPANY

Everyone knows this shiny red beetle with the black dots on its back. It's a ladybug! Ladybugs can also be black with red dots, and some are orange with yellow dots. Some have no dots at all. There are many kinds of ladybugs, and they are all welcome in the garden.

Male and female ladybugs mate in spring. After mating, a female lays bright yellow eggs on a leaf. In about a week, a tiny larva hatches from each egg.

Ladybug larvae look nothing like adult ladybugs. The larvae are mostly black, and their bodies have tiny spines and many segments. As soon as they hatch, the hungry larvae go off searching for food.

Like their parents, ladybug larvae love to eat aphids. A larva uses its sharp jaws to crush an aphid's body. Then it sucks out the aphid's juices.

Aphids are tiny insects that damage crops and gardens by feeding on plant juices. They multiply quickly, but one ladybug larva can eat hundreds of aphids. That's why farmers and gardeners like ladybugs so much!

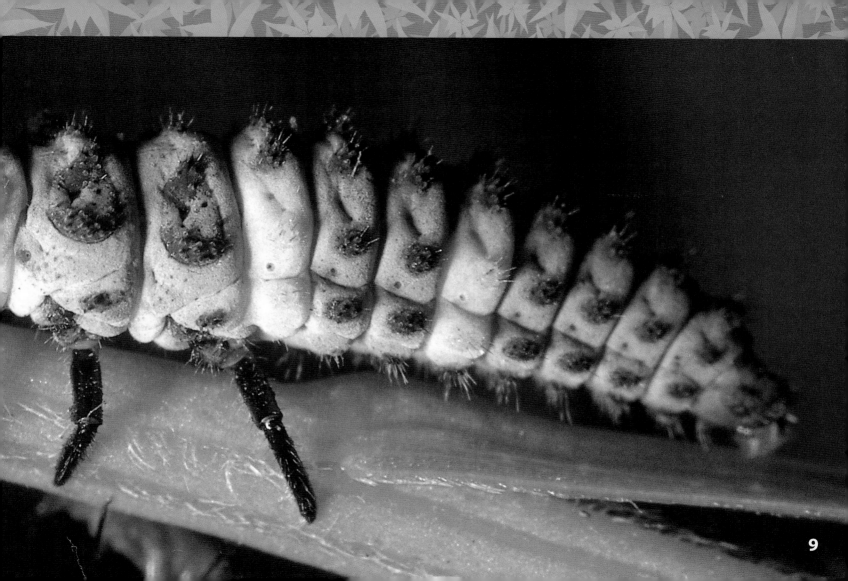

9

As a larva's body grows bigger and bigger, its skin does not. When the skin becomes too tight, the larva molts, or sheds the skin. It has new skin underneath.

Right after molting, the larva's legs are light-colored, but they soon turn black.

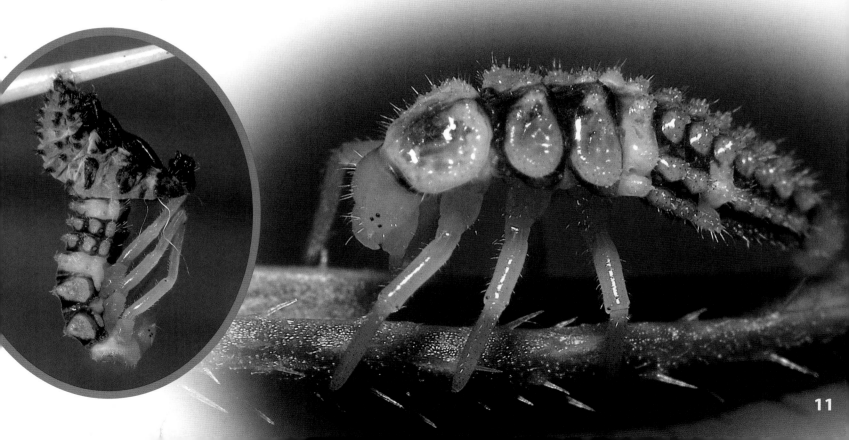

A larva molts three or four times before beginning the next stage of its life. The last time it molts, it cements itself to a leaf. This time, it has a hard, dry casing under its old skin. The larva is now a pupa. Inside the casing, amazing changes are taking place.

After about a week, the pupa splits open, and an adult ladybug crawls out! Its body is soft and moist — and it is yellow, with no dots.

The adult ladybug rests as its body hardens and its colors change. Its hard front wings turn red and black. These wings rest over the ladybug's back like a shell. They pop up when the ladybug flies off in search of aphids.

When cold weather arrives, ladybugs look for shelter. They crawl into a pile of leaves or under a moss-covered rock and hibernate, or sleep through the winter, in a red-and-black heap.

In spring, the ladybugs come out of the shelter and look for mates. Then the ladybug life cycle begins again.

Can you put these steps in the life cycle of a ladybug in order?

Answer

aphids: tiny, licelike insects that damage plants by sucking out their juices.

beetle: an insect with two pairs of wings — hard front wings rest on top of and protect thinner back wings.

cements: fastens or attaches with a soft, sticky substance that hardens when it dries.

hatches: comes, or breaks, out of an egg.

hibernate: go through winter in a sleeplike state.

larva, larvae (pl): the wingless, wormlike form of an insect when it first hatches from an egg.

mate (v): join male and female cells together to produce young; (n) either the male or female in a pair of animals that join to produce young.

moist: a little wet; damp.

molts: sheds an outer covering of skin, feathers, or fur before growing a new one.

moss: tiny green plants that grow close together, forming a velvety covering on rocks, trees, and soil in damp, shady places.

pupa: the part of an insect's life when a larva is in a protective casing, changing into an adult.

segments: the separate parts or sections into which something is divided.

spines: stiff, sharp, hairlike growths that stick out like thorns on an animal's body.

stage: a particular time period or point of development in an animal's or plant's growth.

ACTIVITIES

Gardener's Best Friend

Gardeners love ladybugs because they eat the aphids that damage their plants. Some people even buy ladybugs to put into their gardens. Visit a garden center and look for products related to ladybugs. Some companies, for example, sell ladybug houses that provide shelter for ladybugs during the winter.

Seeing Spots

Look in an insect book at pictures of different species, or kinds, of ladybugs. Count the number of dots on each species. Which species has the most dots? Make a list of the species you find and write down the number of dots on each one. Then put the numbers in order to see if any are missing in the lineup. For any missing numbers, draw a ladybug with that many dots and give each new species a "scientific" name.

Ladybug, Ladybug

Ask an adult to cut an egg-shaped piece of Styrofoam in half, the long way, so you will have two pieces that look like the bodies of ladybugs. Paint each piece red, orange, or yellow and paint a dark line down the back to show where the ladybug's folded wings meet. Now paint on some dots and glue on eyes. Then add pipe-cleaner legs and antennae, and your ladybugs are ready to "fly away home."

Beetle-mania

Ladybugs belong to a huge group of insects called beetles. In fact, there are 300,000 species, or kinds, of beetles! Find a book or a web site that shows many kinds of beetles. Make a list of all the features beetles have in common. Then invent a new beetle with those features — and add a few new features from your imagination!

More Books to Read

Bright Beetle. Rick Chrustowski (Henry Holt)
The Ladybug. Sabrina Crewe (Raintree Steck-Vaughn)
The Ladybug and Other Insects. Pascale DeBourgoing (Scholastic)
Ladybugology. Backyard Buddies (series). Michael Elsohn Ross (Carolrhoda Books)
Ladybugs and Beetles. Looking at Minibeasts (series). Sally Morgan (Thameside Press)
A Ladybug's Life. Nature Upclose (series). John Himmelman (Children's Press)

Videos

Bug City: Ladybugs & Fireflies. (Schlessinger Media)
The Ladybird Beetle. Animal Families for Children (series). (Library Video)
See How They Grow: Insects & Spiders. (Sony Music)

Web Sites

www.denniskunkel.com/PublicHtml/WANTED/MUGS/IndexMugs.html
www.geocities.com/SoHo/Coffeehouse/7422/nia/lbug.html
www.parkhere.org/kidslbug.htm

Some web sites stay current longer than others. For additional web sites, use a good search engine to locate the following topics: *aphids, beetles, gardens, insects,* and *ladybugs.*

INDEX